Stress Management

Monique Joiner Siedlak

©2018 Monique Joiner Siedlak

All rights reserved. This book or parts thereof may not be reproduced in any form, stored in any retrieval system, or transmitted in any form by any means—electronic, mechanical, photocopy, recording, or otherwise—without prior written permission of the publisher, except as provided by United States of America copyright law.

Printed in the United States of America

ISBN-13: 978-1948834018

ISBN-10: 1948834014

www.oshunpublications.com

Disclaimer

All the material contained in this book is provided for educational and informational purposes only. No responsibility can be taken for any results or outcomes resulting from the use of this material. While every attempt has been made to provide information that is both accurate and effective, the author does not assume any responsibility for the accuracy or use/misuse of this information.

Cover design by Monique Joiner Siedlak

Cover image by Pixabay.com

Logo design by Monique Joiner Siedlak

Logo image by Pixabay.com

Other Books in the Series

Manifesting With the Law of Attraction

Table of Contents

Introduction	i
Chapter One: What Is Stress?	1
Chapter Two: Causes of Stress	5
Chapter Three: Signs and Symptoms of Stress	15
Chapter Four: Effects of Stress on Your Health	25
Chapter Five: How to Cope With Stress	29
Chapter Six: Reducing the Stress in Your Life	35
Chapter Seven: Importance of Stress Management	39
Chapter Eight: Effective Stress Management Techniques	47
Chapter Nine: Choose How to React To Stress	55
Conclusion	61

Introduction

Typical living now is full of stress. During today's face paced world whenever you notice even the slightest part of pressure to act or need to react, be it positive or negative, it is known as stress.

Normally stress by itself is not dangerous, but if it becomes constant or especially powerful, stress can contribute to a complete spectrum of acute physical issues. Long-term stress and the issues related with it have many seeking for alternatives to deal with the stress.

Someone who is determined can deal with stress. In investigating the strongest approaches to handle stress, it will be influenced by the person and the type of stress they encounter.

Every now and then directly dealing with some types of stress might work, but in alternative circumstances, the direct approach is practically impossible. Typically, managing stress must start with a mindful choice to do so.

ii/STRESS MANAGEMENT

Nowadays are quite a few different ways to deal with stress and practically anybody can do it. Many times to secure complete improvement a mixture of methods will succeed the desired outcomes.

Stress management can start with change. A bad career, an imperfect relationship or other influences can be changed helping you deal with the stress connected with the environment.

It is not at all times the simplest way to manage stress by creating a change in your life, however in severe circumstances, it may well be your only choice. If a principal change to help cope with stress is not available, smaller simpler steps might be the answer.

A number of the smaller but possibly bigger changes could include making some relaxation time into your hectic day. After lunch, you can take a walk. Find a favorite location and sit quietly for a while. Play a motivating or uplifting audio whether it is music or a book in your car during your commute.

Stress management is the utilization of practices to either cut down or develop resilience to stress. It is the most efficient when performed habitually.

Managing stress means our ability to keep control when people, situations and occasions make too many demands on us. It is a key to happiness. It is your ability to manage the pressures you feel at work as well as at home. It is about knowing your limits.
Reduce the effect of stress by learning a number of relaxation

approaches. Meditation, deep breathing exercises, or even yoga, can be valuable in teaching you to relax. Directing the mind on whatever is important to you can be a powerful first step in minimizing the impact of stressful influences.

As a final point, you may discover the best technique will require professional therapy. In this book, you will learn methods to best contend with stress and effective steps to work throughout your stress.

Stress management every so often is not as simple as it sounds. However, if you create a deliberate choice to make the needed adjustments and learn to relax you'll encounter not as much stress in your existence and be better prepared to handle with whatever life hurls at you.

Let's begin.

Chapter One
What Is Stress?

Stress refers to the tension from the struggle between our outside environment and us, contributing to physical and emotional stress. In our fast-paced life, whether you are a busy adult or a student, it is not possible to exist without stress.

Hence, it is obvious that some form of good stress can incorporate more color and animation to our ways of life. The existence of a deadline, for illustration, can force us to create the utmost of our time and make higher efficiency. It is vital to keep in the observance, as stress management means to managing stress to our favor, and not on wiping out the existence of stress in our existence.

Alternatively, negative stress can give rise to mental in addition to physical strain. The person will go through symptoms such as headaches, tensions, irritability and in severe circumstances, heart palpitations.

2/STRESS MANAGEMENT

Therefore, despite the fact that some stress could be seen as an encouraging influence, it is necessary to manage stress levels with the intention of it not having a harmful effect on your wellbeing and relationships.

A portion of managing these stress levels consists of learning about in what way stress can influence you emotionally and physically, in addition to how to recognize if you are functioning at your peak stress level or if you are going through negative stress.

This understanding will help you recognize when you want to get a break, or maybe seek professional assistance. It is still your initial step on the way to developing ways of managing your stress levels.

Modern day stresses may take the form of financial needs or emotional conflicts. Rivalry at your job and an added workload can likewise lead to higher degrees of stress. Stress is certainly much a part of the Modern day faces paced living. Knowing what stress is, then stress management is the correct way to beat this and have control over it.

In the modern, fast-paced living, many people go through life stressed out, usually to the extreme level. They think that since stress is an inescapable part of our lives and is the result of external factors, it is something beyond their control to do anything about it. Many go on to endure quietly and do not even consider seeking advice or guidance.

Stress is the response and feedback of the body and mind to the demands made upon them due to certain situations or environments and the way the body and mind cope with the situations. The flight or fight response kicks in due to the stressful situation, which is meant to help us actually to get into the action which is best for us.

Therefore, stress to a certain level is good for us, works in our favor. However, in the current modern day life, what has happened is that we encounter or are faced with too many stressors constantly far more than necessary. So much so that our body and mind experiences far more stressful times and hardly any relaxation.

The body and mind does have coping capability but continued exposure to stressful conditions, adaption energy is drained. The result is that stress starts affecting our health.

Stress has been linked to five killer diseases such as heart disease, cancer, lung diseases, accidents, suicide and more. It is recognized that the majority of physician visits now is due to stress related disorders. The visits to psychologists are continually increasing.

Managing stress will subsist of understanding approaches to cope with stress, recognizing the stressors and what provokes them, so that the next time you come across a stressful situation, you are better prepared and will discover that your control over it will be increased over time.

Chapter Two
Causes of Stress

In order to manage a tranquil, relaxed lifestyle, we must first recognize and know what produces stress. Everyone can answer in sweeping strokes and can identify different stressors with which we are all familiar, such as work, relationships, money, health matters, etc., but are those really the factors that lead to the stress or simply the elements with which we associate stress?

In order to truly get stress under management, we need to search a little deeper into our lifestyles, habits and other circumstances to actually pinpoint what truly causes stress in our lives.

Let's take employment, for example. Some jobs are naturally stressful such as a law enforcement officer or firefighter. There is nothing that can be done to lessen the effects of stress in moments of actual threat.

Nevertheless, that's not an issue since it's for those exact conditions that stress is created to focus on. Alternatively, if

6/STRESS MANAGEMENT

you are an analyst, you can be certain you will never die as an intended result of your position.

The stress that follows this type of work is a specific type that does further damage than good. However, what really leads to the stress that an analyst feels at his profession?

Chances are the stress is made by factors that can be managed, unlike the stress of a firefighter that occurs from the outside in.

What creates stress in these types of situations is frequently controllable is specific causes can be determined. Maybe you are stressed for the reason that you have too much work and think that you cannot conceivably get it all completed. Perhaps you have a supervisor that's tough to get along with. In both of these instances, there are elements that can be accomplished.

Quite often, the little details that we do add up to develop into a problem. Maybe it's just a means of handling your time better or having a conversation with a hot-tempered employer. Often, cutting back on work can literally make you more productive due to the reduced stress.

Source of stress changes as we age. Stress may appear up in a child as tantrums. What creates stress in a teenager? A teenager may become stressed because of acne, their body types such as weight and height, peer pressure, school assignments and family conversations.

An adult may become stressed because of their kids, relationship with spouse, monetary conditions, health, work and family.

CAUSES OF STRESS/7

Kids have many causes of stress. They throw tantrums when they don't get what they want. This can happen at any time. What is more embarrassing and stressful is when they take their tantrum in a public place like the grocery or toy store.

Children become stressed when they go to school for the first time, when they fear punishment by adults or their teachers, wetting themselves, and when their environment is not stable either at home or at school.

Teenagers worry about getting along with peers, about schoolwork, fear about being chosen last for any team and worry about their changing bodies. When teens start dating, there is peer pressure about grades, their choices of friends, what they wear, how they look and relations with the opposite sex.

Adults worry about their children and how they will develop through life. Parents always wish their children to achieve and occasionally that pressure is stressful for all family members. Comparing one child's achievement with another is stressful on the child to achieve. Adults also are stressed because of finances, work duties, and overall world affairs and point of view of others. Another major stress for adults is family ties that may consist of your relationships with your parents, partner and children.

We all deal with stress every day. Here are some of the main producers.

8/STRESS MANAGEMENT

Work

Work is a considerable cause of stress. Working long days, and dealing with a huge workload, can allow limited time for fun in your life. You may be experiencing a poor management system, with vague expectations of your work, and no say in the judgment making process. You may even be lacking confidence about your chance for advancement or risk of termination.

Another cause of stress is an undesirable work environment. This can mean anything from working under dangerous conditions, a verbally abusive employer, feuding coworkers, to fellow employees who are making unwanted amorous advances to you.

Are you dealing with discrimination or perhaps harassment at work? Stress can arise, particularly if your company isn't supportive.

If you find yourself tensing up or feeling depressed before you even get to work in the morning, which is a clear indication that your job is a great source of stress in your life.

Finances

We recognize financial stress can influence virtually every facet of your life. If you find yourself continually find obsessing how much money you have or don't have and how you're going to provide for your family, maintain a roof over your head, get to and from work, you could absolutely develop one of several stress associated health conditions.

Financial troubles are a leading source of stress, not just on individuals, but on relationships as well. Many divorced and separating couples will present financial troubles as one of the major causes of their separation. Constant concern about credit card debt, or the high cost of living, can make it hard for some to sit back and experience life.

Family Life

Our family can be a cause of considerable joy, strength and support. However, they can also be a source of a considerable deal of stress. Raising children and managing everything you can to make sure they are happy, healthy and well cared for can be stressful. If you have several children, just keeping all of their individual schedules straight can be a significant source of stress.

When you get sick, it's bad enough, but if you're the caregiver to a sick or disabled child, spouse, or elderly parent, you have even more to worry about. In addition to the physical consequences of experiencing caregiver stress, the negative emotions can take their weight, as well. Many individuals feel irritated, angry, sad, even terrified about being caregivers, as they didn't desire it.

Relationship problems, like conflicts with your spouse, or divorce proceedings, can make the other stresses in your life seem even worse.

Housing

It may be a joyful celebration. For example, if you are moving from a one-bedroom condominium to the home of your dreams, this is still stressful. Everyone hates moving. Most individuals go through the stress from the minute the decision is made, from the initial box is packed to when the movers are selected.

Homelessness, and the issues associated with homelessness, greatly influences not only men and women, but also children and their capability to be successful in their schoolwork.

Then there are the neighbors. Our neighbors can trouble you and cause stress in many circumstances. Some of the common causes are the unwanted noise from loud music and conversation, machinery, traffic, screaming children and barking dogs. There is also overcrowding which can be especially problematic for people residing in high-rise apartments. Lastly is possessing different values, especially for safety, held by neighbors can also generate tension within the neighborhood.

Holiday Stress

The pressure of shopping, holiday travel, parties, a chance to reconnect with colleagues, and family parties can frequently cause the season to be more stressful than cheerful. There never seems to be sufficient time to get tasks completed. Maybe you are concerned about money. You may feel pressure to purchase and give presents. It's essential to see beyond the stress and to enjoy these moments of year, however.

The same goes for arranging your vacation at any time of year. Once you get everything organized, and purchased for, you're by this time not look forward to the work that you'll surely come back to.

Driving

For some, just traveling to work in the morning is a significant source of stress. Even when you anticipate events such as keeping a steady speed, braking and pulling away when the lights change or just sitting in traffic can increase your stress. The excessive traffic, road construction, peeved by the behavior of their fellow motorists, or apprehensive about being able to maneuver the crowded streets safely, irritates them.

The stress created by driving through traffic has literally forced some people to extremes, ending in countless road rage episodes that are linked to a higher risk for collisions.

Dangerous and Past Events

Unsafe conditions will lead an individual to feel stressed. This can consist of being the victim of a violation, financial, physical or social threats can create stress. Any hazardous situation that is out of the commonplace for an individual can lead to either short term or long term emotional or physical stress. It will be worse when the individual thinks they have no response that can diminish the threat, as this influences the desire for a sense of control.

Prior experiences can be a key cause of stress. Whilst any threat an individual has encountered may have happened, the stress of the ordeal can continue to influence them for many years thereafter. It is estimated that around one half of women experience a traumatic situation at least once in their life, and are more susceptible to be victims of sexual attack than men. On the other hand, one third of men also encounter trauma, a difference that it applies to males being more prone to be involved in accidents.

Relentless stress that continues long following a painful experience has passed is generally described as PTSD or Post-Traumatic Stress Disorder.

Image Issues

It almost looks like no one is content with the way they look. Even many supermodels claim that there is at least one feature about their bodies that they hate.

Many individuals waste a considerable deal of their time and energy fretting about how they look and how much they weigh. They spend billions of dollars a year on cosmetic surgery, weight loss programs and fad diets, struggling to make themselves look the way they expect they should.

Considering how much stress we have to handle with every day, discovering ways to deal with that stress is necessary. Nevertheless, the processes some manage to deal with stress only make matters worse. Some individuals turn to liquor to relax and de-stress, but when alcohol use grows out of control, it creates bigger issues and more stress in your life.

Some individuals find food comforting. When they're eating their favorite dinner or snack, their problem seems to melt away for a time. However, relying on food too much can contribute to weight gain, and weight is a significant source of stress for many individuals.

We all have to deal with stress. However, once you understand what produces stress, you can then discover alternatives to deal with it the right way.

Chapter Three
Signs and Symptoms of Stress

Although stress is something that everybody encounters from time to time, it is necessary for you to be familiar of the various signals and symptoms of stress. If left alone, stress can contribute to far more damages than most individuals can imagine.

In modest dosages, stress can frequently offer you the boost you need to perform a certain task. However, if the stress becomes far too much, it can develop into a threat to you physically and emotionally.

In order to get a hold of your stress, you have to understand the various signs and symptoms of stress. While everyone becomes stressed out for different reasons, many of these symptoms are similar from person to person. Being aware of these signs can help you to relax, rationalize and relieve yourself from the burden of the stress.

16/STRESS MANAGEMENT

Firstly, you must acknowledge the fact that stress influences the mind, body and behavior in several different ways. While many of the symptoms are similar from person to person, the type of symptoms each person experiences may vary.

Some individuals may experience, mostly physical symptoms, while others may be strictly emotional symptoms. Nonetheless, it is essential for you to be mindful of each symptom that you may experience.

Stress is a serious issue in the modern world. More than 50% of appointments to visit a doctor are linked to stress in one form or another. One of the major reasons that stress is such a great problem is that most people overlook it altogether; either not recognizing the symptoms or remaining in denial, assume it will pass or just will not influence them as it does everybody else.

Ignoring high degrees of stress is a critical mistake, because it brings to much very severe health and mental problems, including heart condition, cancer, lung illnesses, and accidents, cirrhosis of the liver, anxiety and suicide. Most of these conditions are produced by the bodies/brain inappropriate reaction to an anticipated risk.

The brain sets the body into an alarmed state ready to fight off the threat or run away. This is seen as the fight or flight response. This was a great defense system when the threats were physical and the threats were short term, but in the current world, most of our dilemmas and concerns are in our heads and cannot be simply fixed physically.

SIGNS AND SYMPTOMS OF STRESS/17

This means that your body ends up in an alert or increased state for greatly prolonged periods; this is what leads to the actual long-term harm to your body. This extended alert body state contributes to the manifestations of stress listed below and ultimately too many severe health problems.

Anxiety

Using the office as an illustration, imagine you have not completed your workload on Friday. Due to stress, you may be troubled with images of your unfinished work and how it will pile up on Monday. The anxiety can cause you sleepless nights or worse, rises to an anxiety disorder.

Depression

Emotional stressors like those that break ups, divorce, unemployment or monetary trouble can bring about the stress response. Continued exposure to these situations without being able to find a solution or closure can force the stressed person to depression.

Abdominal Issues

Diarrhea, constipation, irritation and nausea are stress related stomach issues which are extremely common. If your stress is momentary, the associated upset stomach should settle down once the stressful situation is alleviated. However, if your stress is persistent or serious, your stomach issues may be more constant.

There are many natural, over the counter and prescription drugs that can soothe upset stomachs. Your physician can suggest the remedies that are best for you. Some natural stomach soothers include ginger ale or pill, peppermint tea or fennel tea.

Palpitations

The sensations of your heart beating faster and /or harder. This is the same kind of reaction you have when you are excited or scared. You can feel your heart beating more quickly and powerfully.

You might feel some discomfort in your chest, but this does not mean you are having a heart attack, it is simply stress. A few deep breaths and encouraging thoughts will encourage this feeling to subside.

Cardiovascular Disease

Stress causes the entire cardiovascular system to work harder, forcing the blood vessels to wear out more rapidly. More fat enters into the blood stream for energy and this can accumulate in the blood vessels leading to an increased risk for atherosclerosis and heart disease.

Diabetes Risk

When stress occurs, it activates the pancreas to release glucose that increases blood sugar levels for energy. It also reduces the production of insulin, a hormone in charge of storing sugar in the body, and promotes insulin resistance. Over time, this can lead to an increased risk for developing Type II diabetes, which is insulin resistant.

Sweating

Stress and anxiety cause the brain to produce sweat, just as it does during incidents of fear, irritation or embarrassment.

Trembling or Shaking

You might see your hands shaking or your legs feeling rubbery or unsteadily. This is natural and nothing to be frightened of.

Shortness of Breath and Breathing Discomfort

Stress causes our bodies to behave as if we are in jeopardy. Our muscles tense and stiffen, preparing us to run or fight. Oxygen rushes away from our brains and other organs to take care of the muscles in their pursuit.

This may lead to feelings of breathlessness and you may see that you are panting or having trouble catching your breath. Recognize that this is a signal of stress. You are not going to asphyxiate.

Difficulty Swallowing

Feeling a knot in your throat when you are under stress, you might feel like an object is stuck in your throat and have some trouble swallowing. This is merely a symptom of stress and does mean that you will choke. Do your best to calm your muscles, concentrating on your shoulders, jaw and tummy. Your esophagus will also relax.

20/STRESS MANAGEMENT

Fatigue

The emotional anxiety experienced during an incident of stress eventually contributes to mental fatigue. Worry, dread, impatience and flying thoughts wear on our brains, inducing excessive tiredness.

Sometimes we reach for caffeine during these moments of fatigue, however caffeine will simply produce our bodies more stress, culminating in greater fatigue. The best action to do for stress-associated fatigue is relaxing, take deep breaths, and think positive, uplifting thoughts.

Hot and Cold Flashes

Sometimes stress can make you feel hot and sticky and suddenly chilled, as you feel when you have a fever. These manifestations will diminish when the stress is under check.

Headaches or Migraines

Many individuals experience headaches or migraines when under stress. Our blood vessels constricting as our bodies pump oxygen to our muscles cause this symptom. Remember that the pain is a symptom of stress and nothing more.

Dizziness or Feeling Faint

This feeling is part of the mental fatigue we experience when we are under stress. The best way to deal with this weird sensation of spinning, wonky or feeling off balance is not to worry about it and attempt to go with the flow. Remind yourself that what you are feeling will pass.

Illness

If you are becoming sick a lot, that is for the most part stress. One of the effects is your getting less efficient immune system. Stress impairs your antibodies and leaves you more sickly than normal. This is why stress, basic as it is, can create about an infinite of potential illnesses if not dealt with.

Irritability

An individual under too much stress can display mood swings and other characteristics. When left unchecked, irritability may increase to anger management issues.

Weakened Immune System

Because stress diverts energy away from your immune system, it can contribute to more frequencies of cold or flu or develop the risk for autoimmune conditions such as allergies or rheumatoid arthritis. In addition, a weakened immune system is less capable to fight off potentially cancerous cells, so stress can raise the risk for cancer.

Digestion

The smooth muscles in the digestive system are deactivated during stress, making digestion much slower. This can lead over time to symptoms like irritable bowel syndrome (IBS), ulcers and constipation.

The digestive system is full of nerve endings and closely connected to other systems of the body, so the negative effects of stress on digestion can be hard on your overall health and vitality.

Reduced Memory and Concentration

For a short period, stress improves memory and concentration. However, in the long term, the area of the brain in charge of memory and concentration loses its ability to react to the hormones released by stress, and memory and concentration drop.

Aging

The life span of the cells in your body diminishes in response to long-term stress. This speeds up the aging process.

Muscular Tension

If the body is suffering constant stress, it is sending energy to the muscles in your body. Nevertheless, since the body is not using those muscles, the energy stagnates and contributes to persistent muscle tension, and symptoms such as persistent back or neck pain can form.

Because of the damaging effects of long-term stress, it is necessary to recognize that stress is often more than just a mental or emotional feeling, but a very real physical response in the body. This can help you in dealing with stress as a means to take better care of your health.

Check over the list and see if any symptoms relate to you. Be straightforward with yourself, denial is risky and will not get you on the road to controlling stress. Whichever one of the

SIGNS AND SYMPTOMS OF STRESS/23

symptoms noted could be initiated by other factors, on the other hand, if you if you are suffering from several of the symptoms listed, then you are stressed.

It is essential to cope with stress before you acquire any physical symptoms. Do not believe that stress as merely a mental problem that will disappear, it won't without you taking action to contend with the principal causes of your stress.

Admitting that you are stressed is the first step in overcoming it. The next is to identify the triggering elements that are bringing about your stress and then take practical action to deal with them.

Chapter Four
Effects of Stress on Your Health

Understanding what really takes place when the body is stressed can help you to be better mindful of what's going on during moments of increased stress.

When your body is reacting to a stressful situation whether that is a stressful situation, thought, or feeling, your body goes into fight or flight mode, meaning it readies itself to deal with the stress by either confronting it or averting it. There are a number of physiological developments that arise in the body during stress.

1. Blood pressure, heart rate along with breathing rate is raised.

2. Smooth muscles in the body, such as in the digestive system, slow down. More energy is sent to the skeletal muscles used for movement.

3. Glucose and fats are distributed into the bloodstream for increased energy.

4. Energy is redirected away from growth and sexual function.

5. Memory and concentration increases in the short term, but over time, both are diminished.

6. The immune system is damaged to conserve energy to deal with the stressful situation.

7. Pain signals are weakened.

The brain signals the body to release hormones to deal with stress, such as cortisol, adrenaline and endorphins. On a short-term basis, these physical changes present no actual harm to the body and in a real stressful situation can help you to completely deal with it. However, in the long term, continuous stress in the body presents a number of health risks.

Stress affects not only an individual's emotions, but also their physical responses. When you have variations in your world, you can become anxious and afraid. When you are stressed, you have negative views, emotions and perceptions.

It creates distance between you and your family, your colleagues and your friends. It can make you to overlook your obligations. It can contribute to dependency on drugs and alcohol.

Persistent or constant stress can produce anxiety and can lead to depression and other emotional issues. When you are continually under stressed, the body increases its level of stress hormones such as adrenaline and cortisol. It has not

EFFECTS OF STRESS ON YOUR HEALTH

been scientifically proven that stress is a source of depression, but natural causes can lead to depression.

Each individual is different in the attitude and emotional makeup. The thing, which may cause stress in one individual, may be different for another individual. Therefore, generalizations cannot be established.

There are steps you can do to reduce and sometimes alleviate stress ailments. There are a number of programs available. However, the initial step is to see that you are under stress and then to pursue help.

Every day is loaded with challenges you have to deal with. It could be your work, your children, bills, school, medical conditions, and so on. Chronic stress, if not alleviated, can contribute to medical complications such as hypertension, high cholesterol levels, heart condition, and the leading killer of Americans and can contribute to depression. You need to learn to deal with your stress so that it doesn't dominate you.

Some individuals can manage stress to drive themselves to accomplish goals. This is known as eustress or positive stress. For others, it is overwhelming and if the dominating cause does not go away, each day becomes worse.

When you are feeling pressured, you should select one task at a time and deal with it. Turning to liquor or drugs doesn't solve the problem. It's still there when the effects wear off.

Your body reacts to stress by producing tension. Your neck and your shoulders get tight. You have headaches that don't go away after you have an aspirin. If the stress is

28/STRESS MANAGEMENT

overwhelming, you lose sleep. Your body needed REM sleep. It relieves stress and is an essential coping system.

You have to figure out what is creating your stress before you can handle it. When you are going through the side effects of stress, your capability to react is inhibited. For your own well-being, you have to take control and deal with your stress.

Chapter Five
How to Cope With Stress

Stress can be brought on by anything; it's all extremely natural to feel stressed on a routine basis. There are, of course, various degrees to how stressed you feel, but an individual is going to be stressed even if only mildly stressed routinely.

It may be that you have a career that is really a stressful environment and demanding or perhaps you have quite a hectic home life and children to take care of.

It's no mystery that we are presently experiencing one of the biggest economic down shifts in decades, which is also adding to people's concerns. More and more people than ever in our time are facing extreme financial troubles, which alone is a considerable contributor to stress.

Therefore, with all these elements leading us feeling stressed how could we shift the tables in our favor.

30/STRESS MANAGEMENT

The ticket is to learn to manage your stress. You'll never fully rid yourself of stress altogether, but you can learn how to cope with stress. The manner in which you act to stress plays a significant part in just how much of a grip stress will have over you.

We'll examine a few simple stress management skills you can implement that will help you cope with stress more effectively in the coming paragraphs.

Take Care of Yourself

It is critical to keep a healthful diet and lifestyle to properly cope with and to scale down the effects of stress on your body. Be certain to curb your alcohol intake, avoid smoking and eat a diet rich with minerals and vitamins by frequently eating fruits and vegetables.

You may wish to consider about including a multivitamin supplement to your everyday routine if you are incapable to maintain up a healthy diet on an everyday basis.

Don't Agonize Over What You Can't Change

If you encounter a specific situation which is stressing you out such as debt piling up then take stock. Assess the situation; ask yourself what the worst-case scenario is. Is the worst case scenario really that awful?

What steps can I choose to make the situation better? Work towards results, but don't allow yourself to become self-defeated and decide not to allow it to lead to your stress and concern.

In work, stress is generally accompanied with the requirements of the career or with job and family inequality. To avoid weariness, try one of the ensuing methods:

Talk With Relatives and Dear Friends

Sometimes it can be tough to reach out for support, after all we have dignity, but there's no loss in confessing in someone you know and trust and sharing your concerns.

We all need that shoulder to lean on from time to time. It's completely acceptable to reach out for support when you're buckling under pressure. By speaking about your troubles with others, you'll have a third eye perspective of concepts and more than likely some sensible advice.

Perhaps you have people around you who could step in and help free you of your chores and current tasks. Parents and friends who can babysit the children here and there or perhaps getting people in your family involved in duties. You shouldn't be required to bear the torch of burden single handedly, especially if you're trying to cope and feel stressed.

You may also discover that others can provide practical advice that you may not have recognized. Remember, they're not as emotionally drawn into the situation as you are and therefore will choose a more sensible and temperate manner to the situation. You may even find solutions to some of the problems and anxieties you're under by confiding in others.

Take Time Off

Schedule regular long weekends, holidays and time to relax throughout your work year. If you do not have time to take regular vacations with your job schedule, use relaxation techniques in your weekly schedule to help you handle with stress.

Set Limits

Business owners tend to take on the bulk of the job responsibility. Time management is a priority to insure that you are not overburdened and that you are capable to execute tasks in a timely fashion without being overburdened.

Outsource

If you are feeling overworked, outsource tasks to other members or outsource them to another firm to escape being overburdened. Freelance workers can also take care of you with tasks from places around the world, for a collection of tasks.

Mind Over Matter

Understandably, though it isn't always that simple, but it certainly is key to try to manage a positive way of thinking. Your thoughts influence your mood and if you allow yourself to be overwhelmed by negative thought patterns then you're openly inviting stress. Work on providing a positive attitude even during trying times. Being negative about a situation doesn't solve it.

Have Adequate Exercise

It's natural to overlook exercise as a powerful factor for coping with stress but daily exercise can certainly help you take care of your stress dramatically. Firstly, participating in physical exercise brings an excellent means for alleviating your mind of any worry. Instead of fretting on your own concerns and making matters worse, you can carry that negative energy into something constructive.

Secondly, exercise can help you clear that inner stress that can develop up from stress. A terrible day at the office for example, can certainly have a negative impact and make your body to get exhausted, tense and agitated.

There's no stronger way to free this tension than to work out. You may find excuses such as I'm not in shape or time doesn't permit, but even just a fifteen-minute walk will work to ease your stress so there literally is no excuse not to burn off some of that pent up mental and physical energy on an everyday basis.

Get Adequate Sleep

Most business owners are not getting enough sleep. Lack of sleep can influence your ability to focus and can have significant health consequences if not addressed. It is urged to get 6-8 hours of sleep on a nightly basis.

All of the methods are essential to help you diminish the effects of stress on your body and to help you handle with stress that you have from your personal and family lives.

34/STRESS MANAGEMENT

If you need to diminish stress, start by evaluating everything in your present life that is creating your stress and then take proactive coping steps to scale down the effects of stress on your body.

Chapter Six
Reducing the Stress in Your Life

Stress is just a part of life and can be identified no matter where in the earth you go. It's not reasonable to believe that we are wrestling against Fate, chance or even God. Stress does not appear just to make our day unbearable.

Unbelievably stress is a natural feedback to a response made the appearing of a contributing event. For every reaction, there is a feedback and repeatedly, the stress that we have to undergo in life is the stress that we make up on ourselves with the decisions we create.

An individual may be stressed out because he or she lives in a dysfunctional relationship as an illustration. However, this is the relation that they choose to become engaged in and continue in.

In an employment environment, for the same reason, a store manager may be under repeated stress because of work

36/STRESS MANAGEMENT

guidelines and selling pressure. They accepted the position all the same; see that it would be a significant stress position.

Similarly, some of man's unhealthy practices, direct repercussions of an act selected, have produced many illnesses and severe health conditions on. It is to be foreseen that you will most likely have some stress in your world.

What is crucial is that you understand how to spot likely causes of stress, that you minimize unnecessary stress, and that you learn how to deal with stress that you claim you can get clear of.

Life experience is a harsh teacher, but perhaps the finest teacher that we will constantly have. Experience teaches up that some mistakes we create can contribute to very dishearten, even dire repercussions. Fortunately, for us, much of humanity's life struggle has been chronicled in books.

The more you receive from the knowledge of others, the more cautiously you will meet life, and in the end, the less stressful conditions you will be opened to. It has been suggested that hindsight id always 20/20.

As you glance back on some of the poor decisions you have carried out, you may discover now that you were literally given adequate warning as to the volume of authority that stretched ahead of you.

Understanding this will lead to you to become more accurate as you make choices in the present and the future. You may notice that some likely causes of stress are evident and may best be avoided at this specific moment in your life.

REDUCING THE STRESS IN YOUR LIFE

For instance, there may be a new position of supervisor opening up in the office. However, you remember meeting the supervisor and may have seen that she was constantly stressed when she was working. If you are susceptible to excessive anxiety or have a medical condition that may be worsened by accepting this position, then it would be reasonable to attempt something else.

Another case would be pursuing an amorous involvement in a friend. You may already detect some not so favorable traits in that individual. Would your stress level be worsen if you became romantically entangled with this person? Similar questions may crop up in looking at issues of family and entrepreneurship.

Could you be prepared to handle the responsibility of a new position at work, an addition to your family or even the pressure of finally opening your own business? Called exercising foresight, this is how you would plan wisely. Reduce your future stress level by diminishing the potential causes of stress you are going through in your life.

There are many remedies out there varying from the extreme (hypnosis or drug) to the comparably simple. Exercise is one healthy approach to deal with stress since rigorous physical activity releases endorphins. Endorphins serve as mood enhancers while also help with the alleviation pain.

Exercise is also a highly goal oriented activity, one that you can see and feel the benefits right away. It may also promote learning some stress management approaches. Calming yourself in moments of stress is essential.

38/STRESS MANAGEMENT

Slowly breathe in by way of your nose, and then out through your mouth. This helps you manage your breathing rate. Meditation has found valuable as another form of stress management.

If you have more persistent troubles with professional or personal stress, or have frequent panic attacks, then you may suffer from an anxiety disorder. These stress problems should be professionally researched and cared for.

This does not automatically mean that drugs will be needed. Alternative forms of therapy, in holistic medicine or a shift of diet, have found extremely helpful for some.

Chapter Seven
Importance of Stress Management

If you have been contemplating the value of stress management in your life, you are likely to benefit from this practical guide. Stress management is a method that gives you the opportunity to understand how to effectively handle the emotions that you encounter on an everyday basis.

In achieving this task, you will notice that you are often more prone to achieve a positive point of view and mindset. You will discover that you look forward to each day and that you are better prepared to handle the situations that develop your way.

When you are working on stress management, one of the initial actions that you need to do is to spot the situations in your life that are causing you to encounter stress.

You must thoroughly evaluate conditions at work, school, home and even in your social life that may be making you to be anything but calm. Once you pinpoint what you think is the greatest source of stress, you can successfully manage to eliminate the stressors from your life.

If you are capable of getting rid of these elements from your life, it is possible that you will encounter less stress. If you discover that you are unable to eliminate these elements from your life, it is essential that you determine a way that you can cope with those situations.

When starting a stress management system, it is critical to stand back and get a good look at how you react to specific conditions in your life. You should take note of how you react emotionally to these matters, as well as how you react physically. There are several points that you should be on guard for.

If you realize that you are extremely depressed, are continuing through a comprehensive loss of hope, feeling suicidal impulses or physical complications such as breathing difficulties and similar issues, you must set up an appointment with a physician as quickly as possible rather than later. These situations generally require medical benefit to achieve an effective program for dealing with stress levels.

There are many questions that you should ask yourself while forming a stress management program. These questions will help you figure out if you require medical help when it comes to establishing a program that will help you better deal with the actions that result in stress:

1. Do you regularly experience the sense that you lack control of the situation that take place around you?

2. Do you sometimes think that you normally lack control over yourself?

3. Have you been diagnosed with high blood pressure?

4. Do you feel as if there is actually no hope when it comes to the future?

5. Have you ever felt as if you may be better off no longer living?

If you responded yes to any of the raised questions, it is imperative that you seek medical help right away. Answering in a positive manner to these questions normally suggest that you require a bit more than just a basic stress management program.

If you said no to the raised questions, then it is possible that you can establish a simple stress management program that is valuable.

It is necessary to recognize that if you shift the way that you view at specific situations, it is possible that you will look at it not actually a situation that results in stress, but how you see it. If you encounter stress, you must develop a means to cope with it.

You may prefer to count as you inhale and exhale or take a walk or even clean. The decision is yours. The important fact is that the choice you create allows you to cope with the reactions that you experience emotionally and physically.

Stress can influence your physical, mental as well as your emotional health. This is why it is fundamental to diminish or eliminate stress in your life so that you can promote better overall health. Stress has been completely determined to contribute to the reduced health condition and a wide range of minor to major health illness.

Through the initiating stage of stress, you might have become conscious that you develop numerous minor conditions such as headaches or digestive troubles. As your body is frequently exposed to stress, you could ultimately suffer from more severe conditions such as high blood pressure, heart condition and stroke.

You must accordingly take the time to understand about stress related illnesses to fully realize the value of developing a stress management regimen.

Healthier Appearance and Looks

If you wish to appear better, then perhaps you should begin to think about in what way you can decrease stress in your life. That's right, reducing stress can cause you to seem even more attractive. Your well-being and your physical presence are directly comparable. Therefore, you can also look better, if you are healthy.

You must accordingly take constructive steps to diminish stress, and then begin to look better. Some of the factors you want to do to assure such results is to have sufficient sleep, eat right, daily exercise and manage your emotions. Every one of these issues combine for you to stay healthier, have a more appealing image and help to maintain your body tone.

Having Sex

Being close to your partner can soothe stress and anxiety. Sex and intimacy can boost your self-esteem and happiness as the body releases oxytocin, also known as the love hormone. Oxytocin acts as a natural sedative and can trigger feelings of compassion.

Enjoying Music

Music has the capability to aid individuals in a pursuit to feel wonderful. Listening to music can have an extremely relaxing effect on our minds and bodies. It can help make you feel joyful, seductive, relaxed, or if you listen to the incorrect kind at the improper moment, irritable. One of the finest reasons to listen to music nevertheless, is because it can alleviate stress especially slow, relaxed classical music. Classical music can have a valuable effect on our physical functions, slowing the pulse and heart rate, decreasing blood pressure, and reducing the levels of stress hormones. The physical reactions that music changes will also benefit to transform your desires and finally reduce stress.

Dancing

The objective reason for why dance possesses the capability to act as a stress reliever stems from the belief that when the body feels great, the mind does, too. Any type of physical action releases neurotransmitters and endorphins that serve to diminish stress.

Caring For Pets

Pets deliver a whole lot of beneficial traits, as well as positive effects on your blood pressure and hormones.

Maintaining A Understanding Circle of Friends

What takes place if you are hurrying through the bank and run into someone who recognizes you? There is an instant flow of positive sentiment, you feel stable in your neighborhood to discover someone you know and like, and you have shared topics to discuss without taking any extra time or effort to sustain such an effective exchange. Those who have a prosperous social life receive the benefit of having increased meets on a routine basis, also are excellent mood promoters. It is one of the most powerful wellness mechanisms for many individuals to spend time with people you appreciate. They have discovered that regular contact with family members and friends who are supportive keeps them well. They have even discovered that speaking another individual how they feel when they don't feel well can help them to feel better.

Laugh with Friends

There is one stress management approach, however, that frequently becomes unnoticed, and this is laughter. There is some accuracy to the traditional saying that laughter is the best medicine.

There are many forms to introduce some more into your way of life. Useful opportunities are meeting with friends, taking in a live comedy show, or watching an entertaining film.

Increasing Efficiency

In large amounts, stress can draw away your focus. Therefore, when you are released from stress, you additionally increase your capability to focus and boost productivity in whatever you undertake. When you raise your efficiency, you are less prone to suffer from the consequences of stress because of accumulations or loss of time to finish your assignments.

There are numerous practical stress management practices you need to cultivate and beat the lack of productivity. Grabbing power naps at some point at work is an excellent way to refresh both the mind and body, particularly if you are beginning to lose attention. You can also adjust proper time management procedures to insure that all of your responsibilities are accomplished in a timely fashion.

Enjoyment

The better you can fight stress, the more enjoyment you can have. Stress will unquestionably take the joy away from your life; therefore, it is necessary to have valuable stress relievers. Experts advise several practical stress management skills so you can have more fun and eliminate stress.

Keeping Your Stress Level in Control

The capability to live life free of stress is the biggest motivator to shaping an effective stress management regimen. If you can successfully deal with stress in your life, you can have more stamina, increase productivity and appreciate life in general.

Chapter Eight
Effective Stress Management Techniques

Healthy stress management must be an important part of everybody's life. It's extremely easy nowadays to resort to vices and dangerous actions when something stressful takes place. Stress happens to everybody and it has an extensive impact on every facet of our lives.

Therefore, understanding and applying healthy stress management skills in our everyday lives is needed for sustaining physical and emotional health. Each person handles stress differently on the other hand by adopting strong stress management guidelines you can learn to hold stress levels closely controlled and keep away from physical and emotional symptoms that appear with it.

Stress can develop abruptly or form up over a period time. As a result, it is necessary to try to minimize unnecessary stressful conditions by being prepared, handling your time and figuring out problems promptly. This means being reasonable and working out issues before they explode.

48/STRESS MANAGEMENT

There is just so much time during the day, so do not take on more projects or actions that are bound to stretch you thin. These consist of financial needs as well. Turning down or saying no to the requests of others does not make you an awful individual, parent or partner.

It's being practical about your time, your demands and your capability to deal with everything that's on your shoulders. Talk about matters that could change into problems afterwards. It may be painful, but by discussing issues upfront, you can avert issues in the upcoming future.

The reduction of stress is a beneficial stress management mechanism. In addition, it may be varied for everyone, but identifying what stress reduction methods work for you it's necessary for managing the stress that forms up over time. Exercising, socializing and taking breaks are all illustrations of healthful stress management tips that reduce stress.

Still when stress all of a sudden and immediately hits you, it's necessary to know how to deal with that stress appropriately so you can think and act accordingly. Manage this stress by placing things into context, admitting what you cannot manage and deciding on a strategy.

Take a Break

Stopping for food, drink, exercise, fun improves your quality of concentration and is a powerful stress management technique. Eating healthy food away from your work station, having a brisk ten minute walk, a little me time, all ensure that your quality of concentration and improve focus on your return.

Everybody needs sometime throughout the day to himself or herself to have a break. Intensive periods of study, urgent deadlines often benefit from taking a break to allow the thoughts to clear and settle for a while. No one can work flat out 100% of the time all the time and often people notice that the new ideas and observations have come up during their break away from their desk.

This break can be spent doing whatsoever is most enjoyable to each single person, but it is distinctively to relax and alleviate stress.

By performing one relaxing action each day, whether it be scribbling in a journal, meditating, listening to music, getting a massage or even painting, you are effecting healthy stress management practices into your lifestyle to deal with and limit stress.

Express Yourself

Human beings are social individuals as a result it is essential to reveal how you feel. Talk to an acquaintance, family and co-workers on the subject of how you feel, even if it's just to express to someone and not to receive guidance. You will feel better getting your feelings understood and not keeping them bottled up inside you.

Exercise

Exercise is an essential part of a beneficial lifestyle, but it is furthermore an excellent way to deal with stress. When we work out our body send out endorphins into the bloodstream, giving you good feelings, as a result not only does it make us feel better emotionally but physically as well. Think about particular exercises that can reduce stress for instance Yoga, Martial Arts, Tai Chi or Pilates.

Perspective

Having a perspective on every situation may be challenging, especially through stressful moments. However, it's essential to take a step backward and place yourself in the other individual's shoes, or question yourself if it truly makes a difference in the larger order of things. Next, take a deep breath. Taking a deep breath will let you move on with a head that is clear and focused.

Outside Your Control

When actions are out of control, it's easy to get mad or be stressed, but there is no purpose to it. We cannot handle everything. Cope with your stress by learning to handle and recognize that you cannot manage everything. This will allow you to remain relaxed when something takes place that is beyond your control.

Come Up With a System

When there is an issue, the best approach to handle your stress is to create a list of all available results. Determine which performs best for your issue and put it into action. This allows you to determine that you have choices in the time of crisis and by establishing a plan to settle your problem you are dramatically reducing your stress.

Learning to Prioritize

We can become habituated to instantly react whenever there is a call for work or help, but learning to prioritize is an important way to manage stress. Doing the most urgent tasks first helps to manage stress and pressure as it minimizes the need to have people banging on the door, urgently demanding a piece of work.

Seeing things through from start to finish are important, as it can be tempting to start one piece of work, then another and have several projects on the go at once.

This can relate equally at home or at work; starting to tidy a room, then doing a little ironing, then the garden can result in nothing being accomplished and leave behind a disappointed feeling in the evening. If a job task has to be left partway through, make sure they make precise notes so that it can be taken up efficiently once you come back.

Delegate

Let other help and they will take satisfaction in the responsibility become more adept and experienced and may even be in a position to give practical ideas and ideas. It can take a little time and diligence to prepare someone new skills, but in the long term, it generally pays off.

Say "No" Sometimes

This is a practical means to handle stress for several reasons. It causes other people understand that you are busy, allows you an indication that you have some definite control over the nature you designate your time and allows you to concentrate on completing what you're already doing with a sharp, relaxed mind.

Practice Self Hypnosis

You simply need to have a second or two to visit a quiet place in nature, like a waterfall, back yard, beach and revel in the sense of tranquility it produces, or to practice expressing to yourself some positive affirmations and statements.

These are powerful ways to deal with stress, raise your inner peace and increase your self-esteem. Self-hypnosis can serve as a brief mini break at moments of pressure when you maybe need to clear cluttered thinking and access a sense of calm, peace and clear thinking.

Self-hypnosis can also bring an easy and efficient way to draw a line between work and home. Some people find it hard to switch off at night.

They discover themselves constantly checking their phone, emails unable to quit worrying or stressing about the latest project or task. Practice breathing techniques and self-hypnosis as an effective way of letting go of invasive thoughts and setting better habits in place.

Remind yourself to value the separate areas of your life, your family, associates, hobbies and interests as well as work. By introducing stress management techniques, it becomes easier to find a balance between all those different areas.

EFFECTIVE STRESS MANAGEMENT TECHNIQUES/53

You create a better quality of life and establish a healthy work/life balance that brings satisfaction, pleasure as well as challenge and only occasional stress.

Chapter Nine
Choose How to React To Stress

Challenging demands from the workplace compounded by the demands of your partner, children, extended family and other obligations in your life often culminate in greater than normal stress levels that require to be deliberately controlled, specifically when these levels of stress are off balance for a lengthy period.

Many factors lead to increased degrees of stress. Competition in the workplace, which generally promotes self-interest, can result in reduced feelings of well-being and confidence.

Struggling economic conditions and competition have resulted in less stable employment opportunities represented by numerous corporate takeovers, scaling down and outsourcing initiatives.

Commutes to work have become longer for many as cities spread outward. Heavy traffic, aggressive driving, packed trains, buses and stations are commonplace. Pressures of having yourself to work on time for the big meeting after taking your children to school on time only to encounter traffic backed up due to the accident on the highway.

There are many causes leading to increased stress levels, which frequently cannot be avoided, but should be consciously maintained.

Stress reduces your energy and ultimately leads to health problems if not managed properly. It should be no surprise there is an increase in stress related health problems such as heart disease, stroke, hypertension, anxiety and depression.

Often times stress leads to alcoholism and dependence on drugs such as prescription sleeping pills and medicines designed to relax you which have side effects which are arguably worse than the symptoms being treated and can be addictive. If you suffer from severe stress for a lengthy period, your body and mind will ultimately wear down.

Long term stress, such as chronic worry over your job, continuous pressure, finances, constant family illness, or some hardship resulting in an endless grind on your life can sap you of energy, reducing your capability to function and very much reduce the aspect of your life and the lives around you.

Of course, not all stress is bad. Sometimes stress may literally be good resulting in stimulation, which tests you to achieve your full capability. Stress may provide you extra energy required for a specific situation.

CHOOSE HOW TO REACT TO STRESS

This good type of stress, such as what you feel before an important job interview, exam or sport activity, may stimulate you to perform your best.

Extended periods of stress may affect you physically and behaviorally and can eventually lead to chronic conditions difficult to manage, such as:

1. Constantly feeling tired

2. Finding it difficult to sleep over an extended period

3. Losing your appetite or eating too much over an extended period

4. Frequently getting sick or having an increase in headaches/migraines, stomach troubles, or aches and pains which can be explained.

5. Constantly worrying or get anxious, which can ultimately lead to anxiety disorders and depression if not managed

6. Feeling overwhelmed having trouble making decisions

7. Experiencing extremes in your mood, such as aggravation, irritability, annoyance, anger, anxiety and depression which you may have difficulty controlling.

8. Experiencing an increased dependence on food, alcohol, tobacco or drugs.

Where survival and family obligation is involved, there is not always a quick solution or choice for most people.

58/STRESS MANAGEMENT

Sometimes how you manage the source of stress requires making choices involving planning worked out over time or just simply breaking the cycle of what is creating your stress such as taking a stroll at lunch break to escape from the stress you are dealing with at work.

Think about how you consciously manage stress. Don't let circumstances end with stress managing you. Often times you can't avoid the cause of stress, but you can notice what it is doing to you and determine how you react to it.

There are lifestyle decisions, which can help you deal with the effects of stress. It is imperative to know your limits, listen to what your body is saying to you, and do something about it.

Going to work is something most of us have to do and there is generally enough to worry about once you get there. There are steps to manage workplace stress and usually you can and should work at avoiding stress. You may not be capable to fully avoid it, but you should try. Workplace stress often takes place when you feel like everything needs to be done right now.

Ways to Reduce Workplace Stress

1. Focus on one task at a time and ask yourself what is essential. Try not to let yourself get caught up in tasks, which contribute little benefit. Multitasking sounds great, but if you're in the game for the long haul, beware of burnout from too much multitasking over a lengthy period. Work at managing a balanced schedule and don't over commit yourself.

2. Take short breaks throughout the day to clear your mind. Try to take time away from your desk for lunch. Stepping aside from work for even a brief stretch of relaxation will help you recharge to be more, not less, energetic.

3. Always running late? Don't add to your stress by running late when it can be avoided. Try to go earlier in the morning.

4. Resist negative thinking. If you see the disadvantage of every situation and interaction, you will find yourself frequently annoyed and this will ultimately drain you of energy. Consciously try to be positive and find humor where you can. It works. Subtly, avoid negative thinking colleagues.

5. Take care of yourself outside of the workplace. In general, you will be able to deal with stress better when your own desires are taken care of. The better you feel, the better you will be prepared to handle work stress without becoming overwhelmed. Lack of sleep leaves you vulnerable to stress. When you're sleep deprived, you are less able to handle stress.

Conclusion

Stress is a natural response by the body to situations that arise in life in addition to environment, bring about in disruption of what you believe the norm. Things and events that produce stress are known as stress agents. While a body is working properly, it had its own built in stress reaction which assists you in handling with a stressful condition.

By what means a body responds to stress fluctuates. In instances where it is incapable to handle, it can lead to life threatening illnesses such as coronary attack and stroke. Persistent stress can likewise develop in an individual try out with drugs, having disturbed sleep patterns, complications by means of the immune system while it hasten up the aging process.

On the other hand, not all stress is unhealthy for the body. Simply, it is the magnitude and your body's answer to stress that lead one to cross the boundary of tolerance. Remarkably, some individuals find it unproblematic to function perfectly when there is an aspect of stress included, for instance, when they have precise deadlines to reach at work.

STRESS MANAGEMENT

Stress sometimes gives you an edge when doing duties and obligations as it holds your concentration from shifting and keeps you inspired.

Signs of your body's response to stress may be physical, emotional or even behavioral. For instance, one being to suffer from indescribable aches and pains, panic attacks, dizziness, moodiness and anger eruptions.

Separating themselves from others, sleeplessness or even suffering from eating disorders. Anyone as well as the elderly, adolescents and even children can feel the stress.

Nevertheless, stress every now and then does not occur only from actions that are transpiring in the present, at times it happens from events that have been ongoing in our lives for a prolonged period, for instance, years of domestic abuse and violence, going through a separation or divorce.

When one starts to become aware of that they are powerless to cope and that their body response to stress is hindered, then it is stage to seek out help.

Help can be sought out from trained professionals or employing support systems in your life, such as family, friends, associates and sustaining an active social lifestyle is tremendously important.

Also crucial in helping decrease stress is one's overall attitude of life and the capability to discover the humor in life situations, adjusting your schedule to give for extra time for relaxation, decreasing workload and maintaining an all-round healthy lifestyle.

About The Author

Born in Long Island, Monique Joiner Siedlak realized she was a Witch at the age of 12. An avid reader, her favorite genres are Horror, Science Fiction & Fantasy and Paranormal Romance, while constantly learning about the world unseen. Apparently, she has never been afraid of what goes bump into the night.

With her husband, two dogs and four cats, she now works part-time while travelling and writing.

If you want to be notified of Monique's new releases, free titles, and news about wonderful prizes, visit her website at http://www.mojosiedlak.com.

Other Books by Monique Joiner Siedlak

Mojo's Wiccan Series

Wiccan Basics

Love Spells

Abundance Spells

Hoodoo

Herb Magick

Seven African Powers

Moon Magick

Cooking for the Orishas

Creating Your Own Spells

Body Mind and Soul Series

Creative Visualization

Astral Projection for Beginners

Meditation for Beginners

Reiki for Beginners

Mojo's Yoga Series

Yoga for Beginners

Yoga for Stress

Yoga for Back Pain

Yoga for Weight Loss

Yoga for Flexibility

Yoga for Advanced Beginners

Yoga for Fitness

Yoga for Runners

Yoga for Energy

Yoga for Your Sex Life

Yoga: To Beat Depression and Anxiety

Yoga for Menstruation

Beautiful You Series

Creating Your Own Body Butter

Creating Your Own Body Scrub

Creating Your Own Body Spray

Connect With Monique Joiner Siedlak

I really appreciate you reading my book! Please leave a review and let me know your thoughts. Here are the social media locations you can find me at:

Like my Facebook page: http://facebook.com/mojosiedlak

Follow me on Twitter: http://twitter.com/mojosiedlak

Follow me on Instagram: http://instagram.com/mojosiedlak

Follow me on Bookbub: www.bookbub.com/authors/monique-joiner-siedlak

Subscribe to my newsletter: http://mojosiedlak.com and receive a free book!

www.ingramcontent.com/pod-product-compliance
Lightning Source LLC
Chambersburg PA
CBHW071631040426
42452CB00009B/1575